Mina-waasige gii-zaagtoon Ziigwang.
Sunny loved the Spring.

Gii-nimadibi miishkoonsing enji-nookaag.
She sat on the soft grass.

Gii-biijimaandaanan waaskoneyin.
She smelled the flowers.

Giizhigadoong gimewniwin gii-nji-njigaa.
The sky rained down.

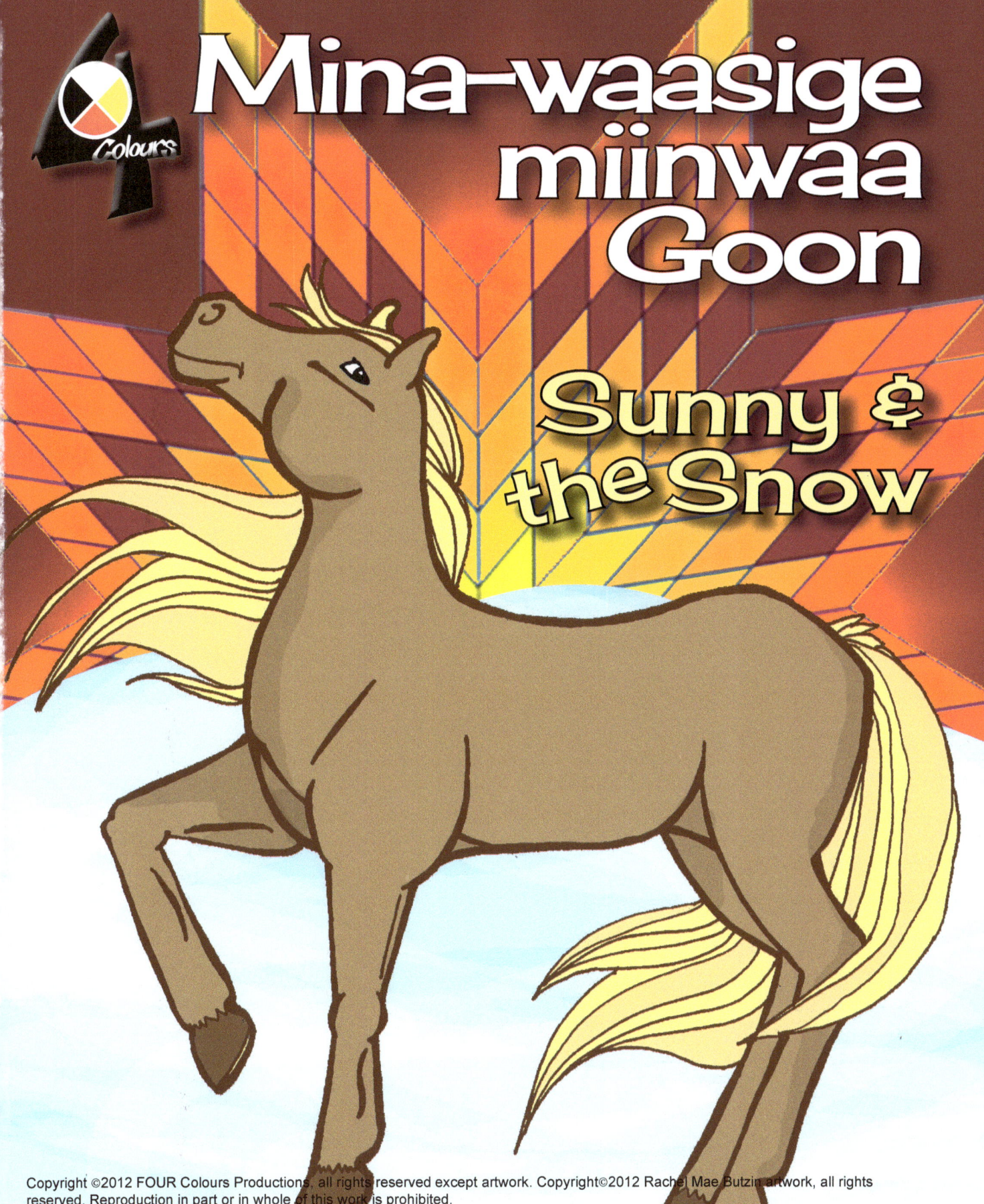

Bezhigoozhii gii-yaa.
There was a horse.

Mina-waasige gii-zhinkaazo.
Her name was Sunny.

Gii-ozaawshkozi miinwaa gii-kii-yaanzo.
She was gold and brown.

Gii-nii'o-biboongizi.
She was four years old.

Gii-mshkoo-gaade.
She had strong legs.

Gii-minikwen gimewanaaboo.
She drank the rain.

Gii-minikwen gimewanaaboo enji-maamowi-seg.
She drank the water puddles.

Gii-mose nbiishing enji-maamowi-seg.
She walked in the puddles.

Gii-waabndiza doo-jibaam nbiish maamowiseg.
She saw her reflection in the puddle.

Mina-waasige gii-mnendaagozi niibing.
Sunny had fun in the Summer.

Gii-zhaa-zhii-baapito megwe mishkoonsing.
She ran through the grasses.

Gii-noodin megwe miishkoonsing.
The wind blew the grasses.

Miishkoonsan maajiiginoon gitigaaning.
The grasses grow in the field.

Kekek gii-gnowaabnmaawan bimiptoonid.
The hawks watched her run.

Kekek giji-mchikaning enmadibijig.
The hawks on the post.

Mina-waasige getin gii-miptoo.
Sunny ran fast.

Miikaans gii-zhitoon megwe miishkoonsing.
She made a trail in the grass.

Dgwaagik ogii-tikiiyaa.
The Fall was cool.

Mina-waasige gii-tibjiibtaa niibiishing.
Sunny rolled in the leaves.

Niibiishan gii-mgisnoon dbishkoo ezhigimewang.
The leaves fell like rain.

Niibiishan kina gegoo gii nandenoon.
The leaves were every color.

Zhaazhi gii-giizhginoon miishkoon.
The harvest hay was ready.

Aabji-gii-zaagtoon miishkoon miijid.
She loved to eat hay.

Miishkoon weweni gii-tikoobidenoon.
The hay was in bales.

Gitige-nini gii-biidowan miishkoon.
The farmer brought her hay.

Gii-ksinaa biboong.
It was cold in the Winter.

Mina-waasige gii-ksaan goonan.
Sunny was afraid of snow.

Goon aabji gii-dkizi.
The snow was cold.

Goon aabji-gii-zhooshkizi.
The snow was slippery.

Mina-waasige gii-zhooshkishin gooning.
Sunny slipped on the snow.

Mina-waasige gii-mgishin.
Sunny fell down.

Mii dash miinwaa gii-mgishing.
She slipped again.

Mina-waasige gii-ksaan goonan.
Sunny was afraid of the snow.

Mina-waasige bekaa gii-yaa biinji-ookaangamigoong.
Sunny stayed in the barn.

Aanand bezhigoozhiig gii-daminowag gooning.
Other horses played in the snow.

Gii-miptowag miinwaa gii-bagwaashkiniwag.
They ran and jumped.

"Bi-daminan Mina-waasige," gii-kidwag.
"Come play Sunny," they said.

Mina-waasige gii-giisaadendam.
Sunny was sad.

Mina-waasige gii-gindaan dibaajimowin mzinigan.
Sunny read the sign.

Maanda mibogoowin gii-mnaadendaagwod.
The ride was an honor.

Mina-waasige gii-nendam ji-niigan mbogwod wiin.
Sunny wanted to lead the ride.

Maanda mibogoowin nji-wiinwaa bemaadizijig.
The ride was for her people.

Mina-waasige gii-gsaan goonan.
Sunny was afraid of the snow.

Gii-gnowaabmaan bezhigoozhiin.
She looked at the horses.

Bezhigoozhiig gii-kwejtoonaawaa.
The horses were practicing.

Bezhigoozhiig gii-yaawag gooning.
The horses were in the snow.

Mina-waasige gii-kwejimaan getzinjin,
Sunny asked the Elder,

"Wenesh enji-gsaag goon?"
"Why am I afraid of the snow?"

Getzid gii-kida, "Gwasaa na goon? Maagiiye"
The Elder said, "Are you afraid of the snow? Or"

"Gzegiz na wii-mgishnan gooning?"
"Are you afraid of falling in the snow?"

Zaasgokwaadenh gii-mkowendaan maanda.
Frybread thought about this.

Getzid gii-kida, "Goon eta goon aawi."
The Elder said, "The snow is just snow."

"Mgishnang giin eta."
"Falling is just you."

"Piichin mgishnan naa'aapii,"
"After you fall a few times,"

"Kiin ka-ni-kendim goon gye."
"You and the snow will know each other well."

"Maaba goon eshkam ka-ni-kendimaa."
"The snow will soon seem familiar."

"Dbishkoo kwiijkiwenh."
"Like a friend."

Dibik giizis gii-goojin.
The moon was out.

Goon gii-waaskozi.
The snow glistened.

Mina-waasige biinji ookaangamig gii-yaa.
Sunny was in the barn.

Mina-waasige gii-saagjise ookaangamigoong.
Sunny stepped out of the barn.

Goon gii-mdaweshkaa.
The snow crunched.

Goon gii-baaskaa gsinaag.
The snow cracked in the cold.

Goon gii-negbizo naamiying zidaang.
The snow sank under her feet.

Mina-waasige niigan gii-tikokii.
Sunny stepped forward.

Mina-waasige gii-tikokii miinwaa.
Sunny stepped again.

Mii dash miinwaa gii-tikokiid.
She stepped again.

Gii-zhooshkishin.
She slipped.

Mina-waasige gii-mgishin.
Sunny fell.

"Ouch!" gii-kida mina-waasige.
"Ouch!" said Sunny.

Gii-bzigwii dash neyaab.
She got back up.

Mina-waasige gii-gjitoon miinwaa.
Sunny tried again.

Mina-waasige niigan gii-tikokii.
She stepped forward.

Miinwaa gii-tikokii.
She stepped again.

Niibinaa-nching ebmiseg gii-aanji-gwejtoon.
She practiced for many weeks.

Gii-waaban dash.
It was the morning.

Bezhigoozhiing gii-maawnjidiwag.
The horses gathered.

Gii-maawnjidiwag wii-wiikjitoowaad mibogoowin.
They gathered to try for the ride.

Bezhigoozhiig gii-noondaanaawa gegoo.
The horses heard a noise.

Dbishkoo gii-nimkiikaag.
It was like thunder.

"Wenesh shii-wi gaa-noondimang?"
gii-kwedwewag bezhigoozhiig.
"What is that noise?" asked the horses.

Aankwod gii-bi-mookse.
A cloud appeared.

Aankwod beshaa mtakimig gii-temgwad.
The cloud was near the ground.

Aankwad gii-aandaande.
The cloud changed color.

Gii-kiiyaande, gii-ozaawshkwaa
miinwaa gii-waabshkaa.
It was brown, gold and white.

Aankwad wiin-gii-aawi Mina-waasige.
The cloud was Sunny.

Gii-mipto gooning.
She ran on the snow.

Goon gaataaying gii-bi.
The snow was around her.

"Wow" gii-kidawag bezhigoozhiig.
"Wow" said the horses.

"Gnowaabam Mina-waasige!"
"Look at Sunny!"

Gwejkazhiwewin gii-maajtaamgwad.
The race began.

Gii-mipto ezhi-dibaabiishkoondizad.
She ran in balance.

Gwejkazhewin gii-giizhitaamgwad.
The ride ended.

Ogimaa gii-naaniibwi megweying niigaan.
The Chief stood before all.

Ogimaa gii-kida,
The Chief said,

"Mina-waasige!"
"Sunny!"

Mina-waasige gii-gchi-nendam.
Sunny was happy.

Mina-waasige gii-maamiikwendam.
Sunny was proud.

"Ngii-kendaan waazhi
maseyaanh gooning."
"I learned how to walk on
the snow."

"Ngii-kendaan waazhi miptoyaanh gooning."
"I learned how to run on the snow."

"Kendaaswin gnesh gii-njitaamgad."
"Learning took time."

"Kendaaswin gii-njitaamgad aanji-zhichigeng."
"Learning took practice."

"Getzijig ngii-naadimaagoog."
"My Elder helped me."

Mina-waasige gii-paatoo getzijig yaawad.
Sunny ran to the Elder.

Gii-aabkwenaan getzinjin.
She hugged the Elder.

"Miigwech," gii-kida.
"Thank you,' she said.

"Gmaamiikwenmin," gii-kida getzid.
"I am proud of you," Elder said.

Gii-zhoobiingwe-ni getzid.
The Elder smiled.

Getzid gooni-bikwaakwad giizhitoon.
The Elder made a snowball.

Getzid gii-pagnaan nindan
gooni-bikwaakidoon giisoong.
The Elder threw the snowball
towards the sun.

"Mbe, miisa wi!" gii-kida getzid.
"There you go!" said Elder.

"Giizis nkweshkoowan goonan."
"The sun meets the snow."

Mina-waasige gii-niigan mbogo
kina bembigoojig mibogoowin.
Sunny led the People's Ride.

Mibogoowin niishwaas-giizhigad
gii-njitaamgwod.
The ride lasted 7 days.

Gii-gsinaa.
It was cold.

Goon gii-shpishin.
The snow piled high.

Kaawii gii-waabsii.
She could not see.

Gii-ni-aabji-se.
She kept walking.

Gii-ni-niigan mbogo.
Sunny lead the riders.

Gii-ni-zhoonaan megwe nchiiwag.
She led them through the snowstorm.

Bembigoojig gii-noopnakiiwag.
The riders followed.

Weweni gii-ni-zhiwaan
enji-gnowendimindwaa.
She led them safely.

Mii-maanda dibaajimoowin
Mina-waasige nji.
That is the story of Sunny.

FOUR Colours Productions:

"An Aboriginal and Non-Aboriginal storytelling collaboration creating learning tools for kids of all colours in all languages. Making it FUN to LEARN and PRESERVE languages."

http://www.four-colours.org

A US/Canada Cultural, Arts & Educational Venture

Brita Brookes:

Brita Brookes is a designer & photographer who travels extensively throughout Michigan & Ontario. Brita has been taking Ojibwe for 8 years. Brita is founder of 4 Colors Productions. Brita has used her creative vision to work on a wide range of community based arts projects. Brita has taught Design Studios at Lawrence Technological University and Wayne State University and has been a visiting critic at the University of Michigan. With a strong talent for brainstorming and conceptual formation, Brita is a favorite among beginning design students for her ability to teach creative, intuitive, and visualization thought techniques. Brita started FOUR Colours Productions because she continually heard language teachers and elders expressing that there was a lack of materials for schools and decided she could use her management & arts experience to form a collaborative entity and make a some more materials. Brita is involved in the native community, attends pow wows, ceremonies, events, was a participant in the Longest Walk 2, US Social Forum, has artwork at the National Library of Medicine in Bethesda for Non-Western medical teachings, and has presented with speaker Albert Owl at A-teg 2011/12. www.britabrookesgraphics.com

Rachel Mae Dennis:

Rachel Mae is a graduate of Michigan State University. From children's books to comic strips, her artwork is always evolving and changing. Rachel Mae is very proud of her Haudenosaunee and Latino heritage and uses her art as a way to share her culture with the world. As a mother of two beautiful little boys she feels it is very important to promote language preservation to protect native culture for future generations. Rachel has done designs for Rez Dog Clothing Company, the Dia de Muijer Conference at MSU, the MSU Pow Wow of Love, Broken Icon Comics and many other events. Rachel has worked on "Ayana goes Fishing" and "Birchbark and Storm" books and videos for FOUR Colours Productions. Rachel is also working on a new comic book series to be done in anishinaabemowin. Rachel's illustrations have a playfulness, hip attitude and light and also evoke a sense of warmth and love. To see more of Rachel's work you can visit her web page: www.mylittlenative.webs.com

Isadore Toulouse:

Isadore is a speaker and teacher of the Ojibwe and Odawa languages. He is from the community of Wikwemikong Unceded Reserve. For over forty years language has been a priority in Isadore's life. He has worked at various schools, universities and groups teaching language. Isadore has been a critical part of Anishinaabemowin Teg as their President for several terms. This is the 26th year in Sault St. Marie, Michigan for the A-teg language conference. Isadore's book, Kidwenan, published in 1996 is a language resource used across the US and Canada in schools and universities. Isadore shares his skill of language by travelling to conferences and by visiting schools throughout the nation. Thankful to have retained his language he is also thankful to be able to share what he has learned with others and future generations. His stated goal for language is that "it becomes recognized as a first language in the province."

Shirley Ida Williams:

Shirley Ida Williams is a member of the Bird Clan of the Ojibway and Odawa First Nations of Canada. Her Aboriginal name is "Migizi ow-kwe" meaning "that Eagle Woman". She was born and raised at Wikwemikong, First Nations Unceded Reserve on Manitoulin Island. She attended at St. Joseph's Residential School, Spanish, Ontario. Shirley has lectured across Ontario promoting Nishnaabe language and Culture. She received her B.A. degree in Native Studies from Trent University. She received her diploma in Native Language Instructor's Program, Lakehead University and did her M.A. at York University on Environmental Studies on Language and Culture on Manitoulin Dialect in 1996. Shirley started her work in the Native Studies Department in 1986 to develop and promote Native language courses within the department. Shirley is a consultant and sat as an Elder at Sweetgrass First Nation Language Council, for the Woodland Cultural Center, Brantford, Ontario. She has traveled across Ontario to many Native communities and universities giving: lectures, seminars, workshops on various Native issues including language and culture.